Growth is Mandatory

Amber Pennington

BookLeaf Publishing

Presentation by *BookLeaf Publishing*

Web: www.bookleafpub.com

E-mail: info@bookleafpub.com

ISBN: 9789357214100

First edition 2023

Fierce

My fierceness was born-
In silence.
A wordless blooming-
A hushed acceptance.
An understanding that-
The life I built was wavering
Discontentment festered,
and like an open wound-
It infected me with a desire for more.
A passion ignited.
I burned with a fever-
I had not experienced it before.
Combustible, yet in control.
An untamed emotion rose-
In the ashes of the life, I once owned.
A cataclysmic force-
Closed the hole inside my soul.
Melancholy was dethroned.
Wordlessly fierceness,
took control.

Control

I found my control-
In a cage.
An incoherent murmur,
Turned into an uncivilized howl.
An understanding arrived-
My prison walls faltered.
Like a crack,
My jubilation branched out,
And burst forth with more authority
Than ten princesses possess.
I burned with a passion
Hidden until now
Dominate, and in control
Like a Pheonix, I rose.
A venomous force
I'd never be caged again.
I have control.

Voice

I found my voice-
In a silent room.
A distant screech,
Became a deafening yell.
As a child, I was taught
To be seen, but not heard.
Blurred and stifled I turned into
A shadow of who I really was.
I grew accustomed to my silence,
And the world grew too comfortable.
Then I had two daughters of my own,
And I was tormented-
By the idea, that they too would
Be shadows.
My anguish grew, and finally
Erupted. I stood tall, I yelled loud
"I am here to be heard!"

Self Love

Paper hearts once littered the walls-
Of my bedroom.
Each one-
With a name
Names of lovers,
Both past and present.
Those who left,
and those I sent away.
They were reminders of broken hearts
Of pain
Paper hearts no longer line my wall
There's just one name left
And that name-
Is mine.

Growth

I am but a flower,
In a field of weeds.
I stood tall, but they always
Towered over me.
I thrived anyway.
I grew stronger every day.
My strength allowed me-
To stand taller, and the
Weeds seemed to get smaller.
My beauty and power grew-
But they wilted away.
Soon, I rose above
And peered down at my oppressors
"I knew I could" I shouted
And they cowered in my presence.

Fear

The apprehension-
Of what is to come,
Was too much for me
The horror of everything,
unknown-
Crept in,
Out of nowhere.
Panic took hold.
Paralyzed.
Unable to move ahead,
Yet too petrified to look behind.
The distortion of reality
Created images,
More dangerous than
Most could fathom.
Life became daunting.
I hesitated, debating-
Should I continue existing?

I had to alter my state of mind,
Because the idea of dying-
Filled me with dread.
Who would take care of my
babies, if I were dead?

So, like a butterfly must
morph from an ugly caterpillar,
I morphed from my despair.
I would be-no will be
Unshakeable!
A villain turned hero,
A pathetic coward turned gutsy.
I will stand up
To my fears,
I will stand up-
And BE BOLD!

Feral

I never wanted to be a housewife,
The implication that I was-
Now tamed.
Tamed by a man,
Who held some sort of power
Above my head.
I never wanted to be a housewife,
But here I am.
Although the phrase "house"
Doesn't quite describe the kind
of savagery, I bring to the table.
The reckless abandonment,
With which I "care" for my home,
Primitive, lawless, unmanageable-
You might say.
My children run wild,
Among the wildflowers that
Grow among our fields.
Barefooted, free, unbroken
Living life without societal penalty.
No, I never thought I'd be a housewife-
So, a feral wife I will be.

My Body

I used to avoid mirrors,
Unless I was criticizing the many
Many areas of my body
That weren't good enough.
I'd pinch, pull, smush,
And worst of all
I'd wish that it were all gone.
The stretch marks, the scars,
The extra skin from my stretched
Belly-that nurtured and grew
Three beautiful treasures.
Now, in my thirties, I have realized
These are marks of beauty.
Marks of love,
I treasure my stretch marks
Because I,
Was blessed with children-
While someone somewhere cries for one
Each night.
My body has been broken,
Weathered and abused.
It is evidence of my resilience.
It is proof
That I have lived.

Time Runs Out

Our time on earth
Seems endless,
When we are young.
Days last forever,
And years seem to never-
End.
We run wild and free,
No worries in the world.
Death is a distant thought,
Because our birth,
is a recent memory.
As we grow into adulthood,
Time seems to fastforward-
The days seem long, but
The weeks are shorter.
Months go by, and we wonder
Where did the time go?
Soon adulthood will become old age,
The years will seem like hours,
The months like minutes,
The days are like seconds.
Enjoy the time you're given,
You aren't promised tomorrow,
Today is all we are given!

Where Home Is

I have heard all of my life,
Home is where-
Your heart is.
Yet, my heart is with me,
And I don't feel at home.
I think a home,
Is more than where
Your heart resides.
It needs warmth and love from-
Others (not just yourself).
If you ask a homeless person,
Where is your home,
They'd say it's with their family.
A home is a safe place.
A happy place (most of the time)
Home is where your family is.
Home isn't where your heart is,
No.
It is where the hearts
Of those you love
Reside.

New Beginning

A new start.
A fresh outlook on life.
After years of being "mom"
It's hard to fathom new.
But, it is even harder
to accept the old.

I need a fresh mindset,
A new understanding.
Life is more than,
Cooking,
More than refereeing.

I want friendships,
Romance.
Passions and projects.
I want to find myself again.

I want time to
Do the things I want
And need.

I don't accept this life.
I don't accept it.

I want something new.

Reviving Passion

When I was younger,
I was passionate about-
Everything.
I spent countless hours,
diving into my newest obsession.
Painting.
Writing.
Fashion Designing-
Although that fizzled out,
Quickly.
Over the years, my passion
Has also fizzled out.
Responsibilities.
Bills.
A Career.
They all took precedence over-
Passion.
For a decade,
I have let that piece of my soul
Lie dormant and neglected.
But today,
I choose to revive her.
Allow her to spread her wings,
And her joy once more.

Regrets

I lie awake at night
Reliving moments,
Reliving regrets.
Like a cassette tape,
I rewind and listen again.

I should have said this.
Why did I say that?

Like a broken record,
Every mistake replays
Over and over again.
Anxiety creeps in.
Regret is my friend.

It keeps me grounded.
It keeps me on the
Path to success.
Without regrets,
Mistakes would mean-
Nothing.

Regret keeps me awake
At night,
Reminding me of
Everything I have survived.

Motherhood

Being a mother-
Is the most terrifying,
and rewarding feeling.
You create these beautiful
Creatures.
They stare into your soul,
They warm your heart.
They mend your wounds.

Motherhood is a blessing,
And a curse.
The sweet creatures,
Only stay small for a short time.
Time steals their innocence.
Time steals their admiration
And replaces it with disdain.

Motherhood is not
For the faint of heart.
Your creations will
Break you,
Hurt you,
And run the opposite
Way.

Motherhood is a game
Of patience.
You love them from
The distance they allow.
You wait for them to
To return home.
You wait for them
To right their wrongs.

And one day, they will
Come home.

Love Hasn't Been Kind To Me

Love hasn't been kind to me.
I found it several times.

In high school,
I met a boy and I fell in love.
The key word is "I"
He never reciprocated my feelings.
Instead, he leads me through months
Of pretending.
He took our best friend to prom,
But told me he was taking his mom.
Our Driver's Ed teacher snitched-
It left me to pick up the pieces.

The summer before college,
I fell again.
This time for a man.
Or so I thought.
We found time to talk-
While working at Target.
We went on a few dates, but
He wanted to go farther.
Needless to say, he ghosted me-
And again I was picking up the pieces.

College was a new territory.
I met a guy, who was-
Both sweet and charming.
We continued our romance
Through three entire semesters,
Before he broke up with me,
because, and I quote,
"It's not you, it's me".
Once again I was picking up the pieces.

The story stays the same.
The guy just changes-
They pull you in, they make demands
And they leave you in the end.

No, love hasn't been kind to me.
He sets me up,
Clips my wings,
And watches as I fall apart.

Eventually, the pieces are too
Small to put back together.

A Caged Bird

I once read a poem,
That explained why the
A caged bird still sings.
It was beautiful,
And Meaningful-
Because I know how
The caged bird feels.
Defeated, but hopeful.
Imprisoned physically,
Yet mentally she flies through
The very fields she will
Never see.

Everything Changes

Everything changes,
You just have to let go.
We can't imprison time,
And we can stop ourselves
From growing old.
And we must change as well.

Everything changes.
It either grows
Or it decays.

Days

Some days,
It feels like my
Emotions control me.
I don't have a say
In what my mind
Actually thinks.
Other days,
I overcontrol everything.
I count every breath.
I shut down every thought.
I own my feelings, but
Most days,
I struggle through
Smile and say
"I'm fine. How are you?"

It's Hard

It's hard,
Being productive
When all you want
Is to sleep.
Depression hanging
In the shadows-
And anxiety at your feet.
Every day is a struggle,
Every breath strangles
You more.
It's hard
To pretend you're
Okay, when okay
Is not what you are.
It's hard
Being alive,
When Heaven sounds
So perfect.
It's hard.
Just know that I too
Know it.

One Day

You are going to miss
Them one day.
When they are gone.
Your table will be empty
Your phone quiet.
No one will yell
From another room.
It will just be you.
You are going to miss
Them.
You'll miss their moodiness.
And you'll probably miss
Their messes.
Laundry day won't be the
Same, without those tiny
Dresses.
Savor today and every day
Take the time,
To read to them.
And sometimes,
Actually, play.
Don't let these years
End with tears-
Don't end them with regret.
One day you will miss them,

But that day hasn't come
Just yet.

Tangled Thread

Life is like
A Pile
Of tangled thread.
We spend our lives
Trying to find
The end.
We spend our
Whole lives
Searching-
For the answers
To life's questions.
Only to find out,
No one ever had them.
We miss so many moments,
I know I have for sure.
Focusing on straightening
Out the road that lies
Before us.
One thing I recently learned,
Is the knots are meant
To be there.
Every knot that lines
Our thread
Makes us who we are.

Printed in the USA
CPSIA information can be obtained
at www.ICGtesting.com
LVHW020534041123
762971LV00060B/1139